Consumers

by Grace Hansen

Abdo
BEGINNING SCIENCE:
ECOLOGY
Kids

Abdo Kids Jumbo is an Imprint of Abdo Kids
abdobooks.com

abdobooks.com

Published by Abdo Kids, a division of ABDO, P.O. Box 398166, Minneapolis, Minnesota 55439.
Copyright © 2020 by Abdo Consulting Group, Inc. International copyrights reserved in all countries.
No part of this book may be reproduced in any form without written permission from the publisher.
Abdo Kids Jumbo™ is a trademark and logo of Abdo Kids.

Printed in the United States of America, North Mankato, Minnesota.

102019

012020

THIS BOOK CONTAINS
RECYCLED MATERIALS

Photo Credits: iStock, Shutterstock

Production Contributors: Teddy Borth, Jennie Forsberg, Grace Hansen
Design Contributors: Dorothy Toth, Pakou Moua

Library of Congress Control Number: 2019941227

Publisher's Cataloging-in-Publication Data

Names: Hansen, Grace, author.

Title: Consumers / by Grace Hansen

Description: Minneapolis, Minnesota : Abdo Kids, 2020 | Series: Beginning science: ecology |
    Includes online resources and index.

Identifiers: ISBN 9781532188923 (lib. bdg.) | ISBN 9781644942659 (pbk.) |
    ISBN 9781532189418 (ebook) | ISBN 9781098200398 (Read-to-Me ebook)

Subjects: LCSH: Food habits in animals--Juvenile literature. | Animal feeding behavior--Juvenile literature.
    | Food webs (Ecology)--Juvenile literature. | Ecology--Juvenile literature. | Living organisms--Juvenile
    literature.

Classification: DDC 577.16--dc23

Table of Contents

What Are Consumers?

Consumers are a part of the food chain. Food chains show how energy flows through an **ecosystem**.

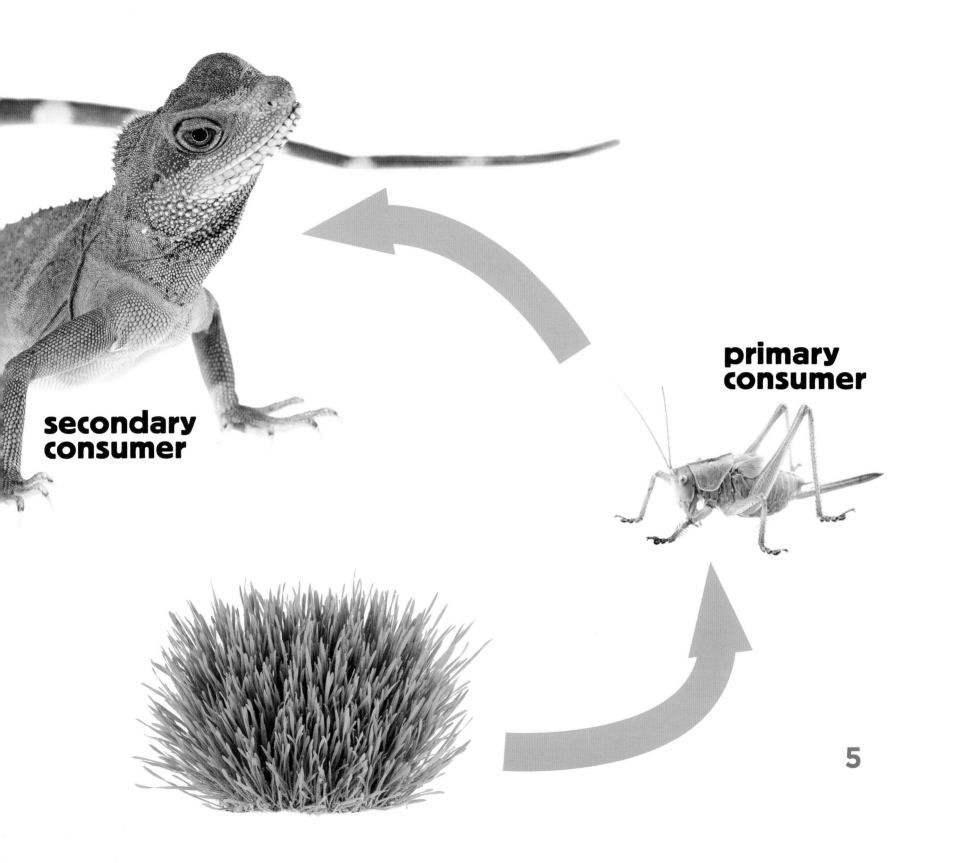

secondary
consumer

primary
consumer

5

Consumers are living things. All living things need energy to survive. They get this energy by eating.

Primary Consumers

There are three main types of consumers. Herbivores are primary consumers. They only eat plants.

9

Sheep and rabbits are

plant eaters.

Secondary Consumers

Omnivores and carnivores are secondary consumers. Carnivores eat meat. Wolves and hawks are meat eaters.

Omnivores eat both plants and meat. Raccoons and chimpanzees are omnivores.

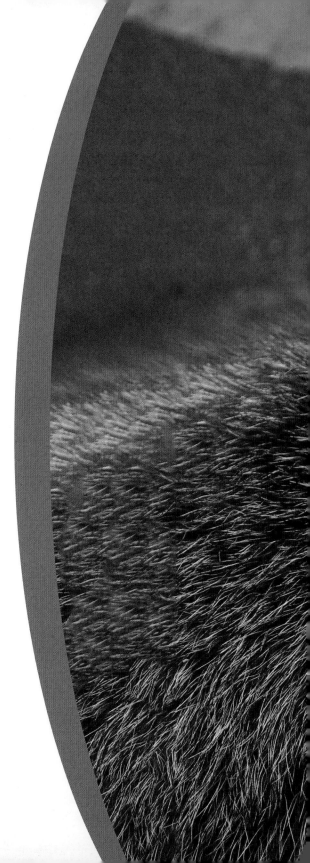

Special Consumers

Decomposers, scavengers, and **detritivores** are special kinds of consumers. Detritivores and scavengers eat plants and animals that are already dead.

16

Vultures are scavengers. They do not kill their prey. They feed on animals that are already dead.

Decomposers help break down any waste that is left over. Bacteria and fungi are decomposers.

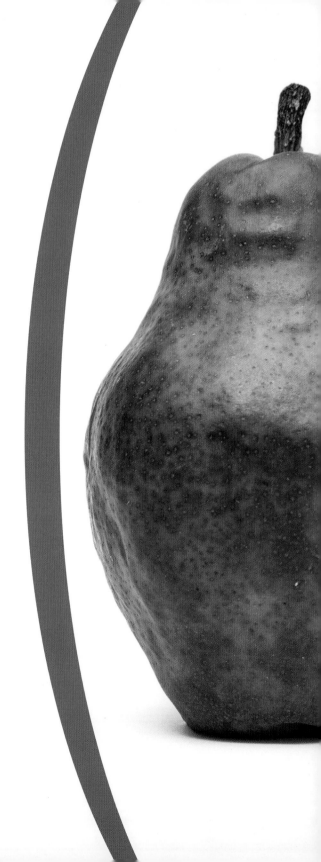

21

Let's Review!

- Consumers are living things that cannot make their own food.

- Primary consumers only eat primary producers, which are plants.

- Secondary consumers include omnivores and carnivores.

- **Decomposers** are special kinds of consumers. They break down waste.

22

Glossary

decomposer – an organism, like bacteria or fungus, that breaks down dead, organic matter in the environment, sometimes after a scavenger is done with it.

detritivore – a type of decomposer that eats dead, organic matter and digests it internally to gain nutrients.

ecosystem – a community of livings things, together with their environment.

Index

Abdo Kids
ONLINE
FREE! ONLINE MULTIMEDIA RESOURCES

Visit **abdokids.com**
to access crafts, games,
videos, and more!

Use Abdo Kids code

BCK8923

or scan this QR code!